Researching Adoption

An essential guide to
tracing birth relatives and ancestors

KAREN BALI

THE FAMILY HISTORY PARTNERSHIP

Published by
The Family History Partnership
57 Bury New Road
Ramsbottom, Bury
Lancashire BL0 0BZ

First published 2015

ISBN: 978 1 906280 52 9

Printed and bound by
TJ International
Trecerus Industrial Estate
Padstow, Cornwall PL28 8RW

Contents

Acknowledgements

So many people have contributed to the completion of this project:

Fellow researchers have helped with ideas and contributed case studies – I'm sorry that not all of them could be included. My clients, by sharing their stories and trusting me with their research, have shown me the emotional, human side of adoption. Every case also becomes personal to me and every successful conclusion a triumph. My friends, often neglected but always understanding, have nagged and pleaded for completion of this project for far too long. John deserves a special mention for his frequent technical support with images. Bob and Terry at the Family History Partnership also deserve a medal for their patience. As always, however, it is my wonderful husband who deserves the greatest thanks, not only for his unfailing support but also for the disproportionate dishwasher loading – Sunil, you are the best.

A note about confidentiality

Adoption is an emotive subject and often a sensitive one to explore. In some case studies featured in this text, names and other details have been changed slightly to protect the identities of adoptees, adopters and their relatives.

Introduction

What brings us to research our family? Perhaps it is curiosity. Often it is also the challenge of study and accumulation of knowledge. Maybe, however, it is something more fundamental - a basic need to belong, connect and account for our kin. An adoption in the family, whether in the recent past or deep in our ancestry, not only frustrates this need but can also greatly hinder our research.

If one or more of your ancestors or relatives were adopted this can be difficult to discover and resolve but it does not inevitably mean a brick wall – there are resources and methods that may help you to discover your natural ancestry.

This guide explores the history of adoption, what records exist for and how these records can be accessed to aid your research. The legal, social and emotional aspects of adoption are also identified and examined here.

If you were adopted the first step to discovering your biological ancestry will be to identify your natural parents before you consider your options. If you want to trace living natural relatives this should be carefully considered, preferably with the support of adoption professionals.

The tracing process, whether your search is for ancestors or living relatives, will almost certainly complicated by adoption. The internet may provide a valuable shortcut in the form of searchable databases, forums and contact sites. However, sensitivity, caution and discretion should be considered where an adoption is involved, no matter how long ago this happened.

As a specialist in modern records and tracing living relatives, my experience and knowledge is mainly of 20th Century adoption processes and research methods. This guide will therefore be most useful to those affected by adoption within their family's living memory. I have also covered the history of adoption before the modern era, but in addition have signposted to organisations and resources, including some excellent books, for more detailed information.

What is adoption?

So what exactly is adoption? It can be defined generally or legally. As a general term there are many definitions relating to the raising of a child that is not one's own. **Oxforddictionaries.com** states that the term dates from the late 15th Century and is derived from the Latin adoptare (to choose).

The Wikipedia.com page on Adoption is comprehensive and authoritative, despite its American bias **http://en.wikipedia.org/wiki/Adoption**

The first paragraph (as at December 2012) offers this description:

"Adoption is a process whereby a person assumes the parenting for another and, in so doing, permanently transfers all rights and responsibilities... from the original parent or parents. Unlike guardianship or other systems designed for the care of the young, adoption is intended to effect a permanent change in status and as such requires societal recognition, either through legal or religious sanction."

In England and Wales an adoption under the Adoption and Children Act 2002 (and other preceding Acts from 1926) permanently and legally transfers parental rights and responsibilities to the adopter or adopters.

Adoption in your ancestry

There are two ways that an adoption in your ancestry can affect your research – these are 'adopted in' and 'adopted out'.

If someone in your ancestry was raised as part of a family but was not biologically a member of that family it can be a challenge to discover their natural parentage. Records might show that a child was the adopted son or daughter of a couple or another person but the origins of the child are not clear. It is helpful if the adoption was arranged through a charity, children's home or local authority where there might be independent records but this is not always the case.

Sometimes, however, a child who was born to one of your relatives or ancestors disappears from records or you discover that they were adopted but don't know how to find out what happened to them.

Each of these situations presents a puzzle that can sometimes be solved (often with a great deal of perseverance). Frustratingly, however, with the passing of time and lack of evidence, some mysteries remain.

If you were adopted

If you were adopted, this often means discovering your identity and origins before even thinking about researching your ancestry. Finding out about birth parents and perhaps tracing natural living relatives is often a priority, but for some the curiosity is more about heritage and history. There are recommended procedures and support networks for adopted people who want information about birth parents and to discover the circumstances of their adoption as this can be a complicated, often emotional, process. Later we will explore the records, procedures and sources of advice and support if you wish to undertake a search of this nature.

The History of Adoption

Adoption – myth, legend and history

Private and informal adoption has taken place for thousands of years. This was often because one or both of the child's natural parents had died or were unable to care for them but sometimes it was, for example, a financial or legal agreement between the natural mother of an illegitimate child and a childless couple.

One of the earliest known accounts of adoption is in the Bible. Moses, after being cast on the river to save his life, was found and taken in by the Pharaoh's daughter and became her son.

Many ancient societies practiced forms of adoption including the Greeks, Egyptians and Japanese. Roman law supported adoption and it is recorded that Julius Caesar's dynasty was saved by his adoption of Octavian, his nephew. The adoption of an adult to become the legal heir of an adopter even had a special term – adrogation – that was different from the adoption of a child.

Under Byzantine law, during the reign of Emperor Justinian I in the sixth century, there was a formal procedure for adoption. This involved a court meeting, which the birth parents and adopters were both required to attended, before an adoption could be made legal.

If an adoption was required to be legal or formal before legislation was introduced, a document, sometimes similar to those regarding the transfer of property ownership, might be drawn up by a lawyer and signed in the presence of witnesses.

Adopted children might be referred to on census returns, wills and certificates as adopted child, foster child, step son or daughter, etc.

One reason that children were adopted by another family was because one or both parents had died. It was common when the mortality rate was higher and life-expectancy lower. Today it is unusual for children to lose both parents before adulthood but before the 20th Century and the growth of modern medicine it was not uncommon at all for children to be orphaned. Sometimes these children were taken into the household of another relative – aunt, uncle or grandparent for example – or raised by friends and neighbours of the deceased parents.

If a natural relative was adopted out of the family this presents a different problem, particularly if another name was given by the child's new family.

Before legal adoption was introduced in Britain in the early 20th Century there were some formal procedures for raising a child as one's own, mostly through charities, in addition to informal family and community arrangements for caring for children without parents. Records of these arrangements can reveal a great deal of information about the circumstances of the child and often yield clues about their natural relatives.

Often, in the past, children were not told that they were adopted. The concept of childhood 'rights' is a modern one and it was usually not thought necessary to inform a child that they were adopted. Social standards were maintained by presenting a conventional family unit (though often an extended family) and, although family and friends might be aware that a child was adopted, the wider community and the child might not know. At times when the alternative to being taken in or adopted was destitution, with a real threat of starvation, the fact that the adults raising a child were not its own parents could be seen as much less significant.

Even well into the 20th Century, the idea that identity and biological connections are important was not considered that significantly. It was thought to be in a child's best interest that it was raised in a secure home, preferably with two parents (usually a married couple) and that knowledge of, and contact with, their birth mother and blood relatives would be unsettling or damaging. This led to many people only discovering in adulthood that they were adopted, often when they required documents to gain employment, join the armed forces or obtain a passport.

Today, the thinking is very different. Ongoing contact with birth families is encouraged and children are almost always told from a very young age about the circumstances of their adoption.

Adoption into non-conventional families is now also more commonplace. Single people of both sexes can adopt, as can older people and gay couples. A loving home is considered today to be more important than maintaining outdated social norms and the emotional wellbeing of adopted children is of equal importance to the provision of a roof, food and clothing.

The Poor Law Union

These Unions were formed under the Poor Law Amendment Act of 1834, uniting local parishes of England and Wales. They were administered by a

Board of Guardians, who were responsible for the running of workhouses and giving relief to paupers.

In 1870, the Boarding Out Order, brought fostering of children into widespread practice. Children from the workhouse would be boarded out (fostered) with local families, who would receive a small allowance for food and other expenses. This arrangement sometimes resulted in the child remaining permanently within the foster family, perhaps as an apprentice or domestic servant and sometimes as an adopted child.

An example of an early adoption

Records are often confined to the usual minute books and ledgers produced by the Poor Law Union in the course of its work. At Cumbria Record Office in Whitehaven, however, there are bundles of correspondence and papers of Cockermouth Poor Law Union for one year only, 1878, which contain details of the adoption of Jane Green, a child in its care. It appears that an appeal for local families to board children from the workhouse had been placed in a local newspaper.

In response came a letter from Ann McDonald, a local woman, offering to adopt young Jane. She says *'I think I would like to take her as she is an orphan and bring her up as my own child. I had two little daughters but they are dead. She would have a comfortable home, as our family is small'*.

The clerk seems to have misunderstood Mrs McDonald's intentions, for her reply on 5th January states *'I do not wish her to be boarded out with me – I am willing to adopt her and bring her up as my own'*.

The minutes of the Board of Guardians record arrangements for the inspection of the McDonald's accommodation and confirm that the couple 'would maintain her without any remuneration'.

Arrangements were also made for Ann McDonald to visit Jane at Cockermouth Workhouse. The next letter states that *'I was pleased with appearance of the little girl Jane Green…if it pleases the guardians to give her up to me'*. The minutes of the Board recorded 'having reported very favourably with regard to the application of Mrs McDonald of Thackay Cottage, Penrith, to be allowed to take Jane Green. Resolved that the application be granted'

Mrs McDonald then asked that Jane be placed on a train by the one of the Poor Law Guardians, and said that she would meet her at Penrith Station. Two subsequent letters from Mrs McDonald seem to show that the adoption worked out well. The first states that *'My little girl Jane Green is very happy and is a very good girl. I am perfectly satisfied with her so far. I intend sending her to a private school…'* and the final letter, dated 28th February 1878 records that *'Jane Green is very content and goes to school regularly'*

This chance survival of evidence showing routine administration of a Poor Law Union gives a fascinating record of the adoption of one child, and would be an invaluable resource to any descendant of Jane Green or the McDonald family.

Orphanages and Children's Charities

The Salvation Army, Barnado's (formerly Dr Barnardo's) and the Children's Society are all examples of organisations that in the past were responsible for the care of orphaned and abandoned children. Although most charities started as residential homes for children, and 'mother and baby' homes for single, pregnant women, they also facilitated the adoption and fostering of children in their care into family homes. Sometimes charities had so many children that a drive would be initiated to encourage families to foster or adopt children.

Suffragette Emmeline Pankhurst, a former Poor Law Guardian, attempted to set an example during World War One and set up a home for illegitimate 'war babies', with her daughter, Christabel. She later adopted four young girls from the home. When criticised for assisting children born 'out of wedlock', Pankhurst declared that the welfare of children was her only concern.

Foundlings

The most common definition of a foundling is an abandoned infant whose parents are not known; one might think of a baby found on the steps of a church, in a railway station or a public lavatory. Most often the illegitimate child of a single mother, foundlings were often left or deposited anonymously in places of relative safety where they would be found and cared for. The most famous name in the history of foundlings is Thomas Coram, who founded a charity in the 1730s to help children who might otherwise have no home or care at all.

Child Migrants

The practice that came to be known as child migration is one that has its origins in the 17th Century and it was to continue well into the 20th Century. As Britain started to colonise different parts of the world, vagrant, orphaned, pauper and illegitimate children were seen as good 'stock' to work and boost numbers of white British children and ensure 'racial unity'. Child migration was a sustained central government policy, supported morally and practically by local authorities and children's charities. At its peak in the post-war era, thousands of children were shipped to Australia, New Zealand, Canada and Rhodesia (now Zimbabwe), with the cooperation of these country's governments. This was done largely without the consent of the children concerned and in some cases against the wishes of any family that they had. Most children were between the ages of seven and ten, although some were as young as three and up to the age of fourteen. Some children were housed in institutions, usually religious, where many tales of hardship and even abuse emerged years later. Other children were given to foster families and while some were treated well, others were used as a source of cheap labour. Very few of these children were ever legally adopted and there is even evidence that records were amended, adjusted and omitted to hide the children's true origins. An estimated 130,000 children left the UK under these schemes in the 19th and 20th Century. A campaign by the Child Migrants Trust (more info under 'Children's Charities') has led to thousands of migrants discovering their roots and reconnecting with relatives from the UK. It has been recognised in recent years that the treatment of child migrants was misguided at best, cruel at worst. Formal inquiries have taken place and government apologies have been issued in the UK and Australia.

Adoption and Children's charities, and the records that they hold, will be explored in more detail in the next chapter.

Three major organisations were established in the early 20th Century. The National Children Adoption Association and the National Adoption Society were primarily concerned with the process of adoption, the physical welfare of babies and children and the rights of the adopters. In 1918, The National Council for the Unmarried Mother and her Child (later the National Council for One Parent families, now Gingerbread) was founded by social worker Lettice Fisher, with the aim of reforming legislation that discriminated against illegitimate children. The organisation was key in obtaining equal rights, including the right to state benefits, for single parents and continues to fight prejudice and inequality against single parents and their children.

The Legislation

The legal process of adoption was introduced in England and Wales by the Adoption of Children Act 1926, which became law on 1st January 1927. Successive legislation making significant changes were introduced in 1949, 1975 and 2002. The latest act, The Adoption and Children Act 2002, has resulted in various new regulations regarding adoption including The Adoption Agencies Regulations 2005 and The Adoption Information and Intermediary Services (etc.) Regulations, 2014.

One of the provisions the 2005 regulations introduced access to identifying information about an adopted person who is a blood relative. Therefore, if you discover that one of your relatives was adopted, it is now possible to apply for information about them and also request an intermediary service to make contact with your birth relative. An interview with a trained adoption worker will be required before any information is provided or an approach to a relative is made.

Adoption legislation was introduced in Scotland a little later by the Adoption of Children (Scotland) Act, 1930.

Trends

Adoption numbers climbed steadily throughout the twentieth century, due in part to the growing acceptance of adopted children and the parents who adopted them. Numbers rose steeply after World War Two due to a marked increase in illegitimate babies and in 1949 there were over 17,000 adoptions in England and Wales. In contrast to the drives to attract prospective adopters in the 1930s and early 40s, during the 1950s there was often a shortage of babies and sometimes charities had a waiting list of more than a year. There was an average of around 13,000 adoptions per year during the 1950s, after tighter rules were introduced whereby the birth mother could not sign for consent of an adoption before her baby was six weeks old; procedures to completely protect the identity of the birth mother also began but the rules were overturned in 1975, enabling adoptees access to their records and to trace their birth families.

The introduction of more widely available contraception, together with the passing of the Abortion Act in 1967, would be expected to reduce the numbers of illegitimate births. In fact, it took several years for these factors to have an impact and adoption orders actually increased to a peak of almost 25,000 in 1968. By the end of the 1970s, the average number of adoptions had more than halved to just over 12,000 and from then on steadily declined to a record low of under 5,000 in 2011. Although numbers have increased slightly since then, due in part to recent changes that aim to improve and simplify the adoption process, there were still fewer than 6,000 adoptions in total for the whole of the UK in 2012, which also includes adoptions by relatives and step-parents (source – Office for National Statistics).

Adoption in your ancestry

There are many ways that you might discover an adoption in your ancestry – an inconsistency in records, a child who mysteriously appears in records but for whom no birth or baptism record can be found, or a child who disappears from records but does not appear to have died.

Sometimes there are clues in usual research resources – the words adopted, foster or even step before the usual son, daughter or child on census returns, certificates, parish registers or wills, for example.

If you find that one of your ancestors was adopted, you might hope to find a record of his or her natural parents. For some the blood line is the only important one and identifying actual ancestors whose DNA they have inherited is what genealogy is all about. For others, however, family research is much more than this – it is about exploring connections between people who have shaped our lives in some way and, while the genes have not been inherited the influence and values of those who have gone before us is equally important. This carefully considered definition of genealogy sums it up nicely:

> *Genealogy is… the study of family relationships, including blood relationships, official relationships and legal relationships, based on biological proof, recorded vital events and legal documents.*
> **www.tamurajones.net**

The adoption of a parent or recent ancestor
An adoption within the last hundred years might not be in the living memory of the researcher but can still be very personal and might have affected the life of a close relative. If you are told or discover that your parent, grandparent or great grandparent was adopted this need not mean your research comes to a halt before it really gets started.

Here is a typical example of a hitherto unknown 'adoption' that was encountered during some routine family history research:

Tarna wanted to find out more about her grandmother's maternal family but had stumbled soon after the first hurdle. The facts were minimal and her very elderly Granny's memory was poor – all she knew was that her mother had died young.

Granny, Rose Lilian Carroll, was born in Greeenwich on Boxing Day 1916, the daughter of Arthur William Carroll, a labourer, and his wife Louisa nee Newell.

Sadly, Louisa Carroll died of TB in February 1918, when little Rose was just over a year old. Arthur remarried and had more children but Rose didn't remember her mother, who was rarely talked about.

Amongst Granny's documents was the marriage certificate of her parents. Faded, folded and much-handled, it was the only clue to Louisa's origins. The marriage took place in Greenwich Register Office in June 1911; the certificate stated that Louisa Newell was aged 24 of 90 Douglas Street, Deptford and her father was John Newell, a coachman.

However, when Tarna searched the 1911 census (taken just two months before the marriage in April 1911) for Louisa Newell as a single woman, she could not find her.

Tarna applied to the General Register Office for Louisa's birth certificate stating all of the information that she knew – Louisa's date of birth and her father's name – and enclosing a copy of the marriage certificate. The search was negative. Despite querying the result, the birth record of Louisa could definitely not be found. At this stage Tarna requested professional assistance.

One helpful research rule is 'go back to come forward'. Louisa couldn't be found on the 1911 census, but what about earlier censuses? Looking at the 1901 census, Louisa and family were found easily and nothing seemed amiss. John Newell, a coachman, lived at Tanners Hill, Deptford, with his wife, 'Melvinia' and their daughters, Ethel and Louisa. All were born in Deptford (all census images courtesy of **Ancestry.co.uk**).

The mother's unusual forename, although there were variations in spelling, accelerated the location of the Newells on previous and subsequent census returns:

The census of 1891 provided the first clue that not all was as it seemed. John and 'Malvina', at that time living at 10 Victory Road, Deptford, had just one daughter – Ethel Newell, aged 8. Also living in the household was 'Louisa Baker', whose relationship to the household head was recorded as 'adopted'.

Checking the 1911 census again, Louisa was there all along, living with her adopted parents at 90 Douglas Street, Deptford, the address recorded on her marriage certificate. However, it was stated that John and 'Milvina' Newell, married for 38 years, had only one daughter. The young woman who would marry Alfred Carroll two months later, was recorded as Louisa Baker, a 'boarder'.

The marriage certificate of 'Louisa Newell'. © Crown copyright.

1901 England Census – RG13; Piece: 534; Folio: 146; Page: 2.

15

1891 England Census - RG12; Piece: 501; Folio: 36; Page: 14; GSU roll: 6095611.

1911 England Census - RG14; Piece: 2629.

BAPTISMS solemnized in the Parish of St John, Deptford in the County of Kent in the year One thousand eight hundred and eighty eight

When Baptized.	Child's Christian Name.	Parents' Names. Christian.	Parents' Names. Surname.	Abode.	Quality, Trade, or Profession.	By whom the Ceremony was performed.
18 88 Nov 7	Louisa Osborn	Leonora Julia E.I. Anne	Baker	Victory Street	Single woman	J S Walsh Curate

No. 874

London Metropolitan Archives, Deptford St John, Register of Baptisms, p75/jn, Item 003 (Courtesy of Ancestry.co.uk).

The marriage certificate of Julia Baker, 1890.

© Crown copyright.

Solving the mystery of Louisa's missing birth record was just the beginning of a long search for her origins. According to her age on census returns and her marriage certificate she was born around 1887, but there were numerous entries in birth indexes for girls called Louisa Baker born around the right time, many of them in London. Only two, however, were registered in the district of Greenwich, which contained the area of Deptford. Examining these, one promising candidate was Louisa Osborne Baker, born 22nd October 1886, the illegitimate daughter of Julia Baker, a domestic servant. The birth was registered by 'C Baker' of 91 Oscar Street, Deptford, where the child was born. The task of making the connection between Louisa Osborn Baker and Louisa Newell proved to be relatively straightforward. Almost all children, even illegitimate ones, were baptised at that time – it was just the social norm. Baptisms for parishes in Deptford were searched and, in the parish of St John, on 7th November 1888, a full two years after she was born, Louisa Osborn (sic), daughter of Julia Baker, was baptised. Louisa's abode was recorded as 10 Victory Road, Deptford, the address where the Newells were living at the time of the 1891 census.

Having confirmed who Louisa's mother was, further research was then undertaken to discover more about Julia Baker. Searching for her birth without knowing her age was not an option – the name was just too common – and there were no obvious candidates on the census 1891.

After examining numerous online entries and ordering a number of documents, a candidate was singled out. Julia Baker of Deptford, aged 30, married Charles Smith in the parish of St Luke's Deptford, in March 1890. Her father was Joseph Baker, a moulder.

The census of 1891 revealed that Julia Smith nee Baker was born in Bloomsbury, London.

Going back to the census of 1881 resulted in almost conclusive evidence that the mother of Louisa had been identified.

Julia Baker, aged 21 and born in Bloomsbury, was working as a domestic servant in East Moseley, Surrey. The wife of her employer was called Louisa Osborne – the name that Julia gave her daughter.

Further research found that Julia Baker was one of eight children. She and Charles Smith went on to have five children, four of whom survived, and they lived a middle class life in West London. It is not known whether Julia's husband and their children ever knew about Louisa.

Although she lived into her nineties, Rose didn't survive quite long enough

1881 England Census - RG11; Piece: 840; Folio: 42; Page: 20

to learn about her mother's real origins but Tarna found the results of the research fascinating. "It's as if I've discovered a whole new family" she says "and I would love to meet Julia's relatives one day".

This case also highlights the misinformation and inconsistencies that can occur in historical records. Before the tighter controls of centralised and computerised records, information that was recorded could be inaccurate, adjusted, partly true or completely false. It is important to remember that the information recorded, even on official documents, cannot always be relied on as accurate.

Records and resources for adoption research

The Adopted Children Register (ACR)

The General Register Office at Southport holds and maintains the Adopted Children Register, containing details of adoption orders that were authorised in courts in England and Wales since January 1927. A certified copy of an entry from this register can be issued from the register, which is the equivalent of a birth certificate (see page 38 for an example of an adoption certificate). The register itself is not available for public consultation but copies of individual entries can be requested.

The ACR index contains very limited information – the child's adoptive name, year of adoption (not birth), entry number and volume number. The index is available on microfiche to be searched at a few key repositories –

- Birmingham Central Library
- Bridgend Reference and Information Library
- City of Westminster Archives Centre
- Manchester City Library
- Newcastle City Library
- Plymouth Central Library
- The British Library

There are no adoption indexes online.

To obtain a copy of a register entry (for children over 18 only) you will need to supply the details from the index, including volume and page number and the child's date of birth. If the index references are not known the names of the adoptive parents must also be supplied.

The General Register Office faq page on adoption certificates is very useful: **https://www.gro.gov.uk/gro/content/certificates/faqs-adoption.asp**

The most common records used for family history research can contain information about adoptions both formal and informal. There are numerous books, research guides and online resources for researching your family history, a few of which are listed in 'Bibliography, Resources and Further Reading' at the end of this book, but here is a brief overview of the main ones.

Birth, marriage and death records

Births, marriages, deaths and civil partnerships are recorded in the registration district or sub-district where the event took place. Although usually this is also where the people lived this is not necessarily the case, it is the district where they were born, married or died. Registers for each life event are completed at the local register office and original copies are kept there. If you know the registration district that a birth, marriage or death took place in you can contact the register office for that district. You will need full details of the event – name, place and date – to do this and be aware that boundary and local authority changes might affect where registers for a particular place are currently held. You can search for local register offices at **www.gov.uk/register- offices**

Copies of the registers of births, marriages, deaths and civil partnerships that have taken place in local districts are sent to the General Register Office (GRO) in Southport periodically, where they are indexed. These indexes, when complete, are made available to the public at a number of sites.

Until the end of 1983 these alphabetical indexes for each event were compiled and indexed quarterly. From 1984 there are annual indexes. Copies of indexes for England and Wales from 1837 on microfiche can be searched at a few large libraries and archives in England, including Manchester, Birmingham and Westminster. However, almost all indexes, particularly those from 1916 onwards, are now available to browse and search online.

Main websites featuring transcribed indexes are www.freebmd.org.uk (up to around 1970 with a few gaps in coverage), **www.findmypast.co.uk** and **www.ancestry.co.uk** If you are using a private computer you will need to register and subscribe or purchase credits for these two sites to view the results. However, many large libraries and record offices (archives) offer free access.

You can apply for a copy of the certificate from the GRO once you have found a likely index entry. The cost of a full certificate is currently from £9.25, depending on how it is ordered and how much information you have about the event.

Find out more about birth, marriage and death certificates, how to search indexes, how to order certificate copies and the information certificates contain by visiting **www.gov.uk/browse/births-deaths-marriages** or **www.gro.gov.uk**

Electoral registers

Also known as voters' lists, these are registers of people who are eligible to vote in households within a parliamentary constituency. They can help to confirm who was resident at an address at a particular time. Older registers (up to around the late 1990s) are held in libraries and record offices around the country, but the British Library also has a significant holding covering England and Wales from 1947 onwards, with some coverage before this date. For more information about holdings at the British Library read this detailed guide: **www.bl.uk/reshelp/findhelprestype/offpubs/electreg/electoral registers.pdf**

A selection of historical electoral registers, including all of those for London up to 1965, is available to search and view at **www.ancestry.co.uk**

Current and recent electoral registers are also searchable online at **www.192.com** and **www.peopletracer.co.uk** (there is a charge to view results in detail).

Poor Law Records

Board of Guardian records can be found in the archives of local authorities throughout the country. County and unitary authorities have undergone many changes in the last few decades – boundaries have been moved, funding cut, facilities closed and departments merged. Where once a county or city might have had a record office for archives, a museum for displaying artefacts and a library for research, there is now a trend for combined facilities, often called heritage centres, or similar. It can, therefore, take some time to track down records and sometimes details found online can be out of date. It may sound simple but an internet search using the term 'Archives' and the name of the place where your ancestors lived can often lead to details of the correct repository. This site has a very helpful list of holdings for poor law records: **www.workhouses.org.uk/records/archives.shtml**

Church records

Church of England parishes in England and Wales kept handwritten volumes of registers recording details of baptisms, marriages and burials. These recorded life events (baptisms, marriages and burials) that took place in churches before the introduction of civil registration in 1837. Many parish registers of are now available online, either as transcriptions or digital images. Explore **www.familysearch.org, www.findmypast.co.uk** and **www.ancestry. co.uk** (charges may apply on some sites but most large libraries and archives have free access) for information about the history of parish registers, what they contain and how to find them.

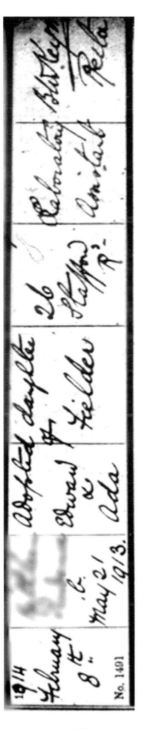

An early 20th Century baptism of an adopted child.

25

Census records

The census is taken every 10 years and released to the public after 100 years of closure. Records that can currently be accessed online date from 1841, providing a snapshot of a day in the life of our ancestors for each decade. The format and information recorded changed slightly each decade but the returns for each household generally show who lived in a property, with whom, how old they were, where they were born and what they did for a living. With this information it is usually possible to track a family through the census for several decades, discovering details about births, marriages deaths and movements of children, parents, and siblings. It is important to remember that information about residents in properties was provided to an enumerator by the householder and some details may not be completely truthful or accurate.

All of the census returns for England and Wales from 1841 - 1911 have been indexed, transcribed and digitally photographed and are available to search and view on the internet. Quality and accuracy varies, however, and whilst information on some sites is free, access to full details and digital images sometimes incur a charge. The information on some sites is from transcriptions by volunteers who have experience of reading handwriting, deciphering occupations and a knowledge of place names. Some commercial sites offering census data, however, pay people who might not have any experience with (or interest in) historical records to transcribe them, which can result in inaccurate index entries. The recently released 1939 register can provide later information about family members, but only if they would now be over 100 years old or are known to be deceased. See www.findmypast.co.uk/1939register for information on content, searching and cost.

Read the guide to census records issued by The Nationals Archives for more information: **www.nationalarchives.gov.uk/records/research-guides/census-returns.htm**

Family History Websites

In addition to providing resources for tracing ancestors and their descendants, some sites such as Ancestry www.ancestry.co.uk and Genes Reunited www.genesreunited.co.uk have uploaded family trees of members and discussion boards or forums for people to request information and connect with others in their extended family. It is very important to not only be mindful that information provided by individuals might not be accurate or verified, but also that the person who has posted family information online might not know about you or your branch of the family. Therefore, think carefully before making assertions of a family connection and be discreet in making an approach to potential relatives found online.

Children's Charities
Charity archives can offer valuable information about fostered and adopted children. It is interesting to note the similarities in the founding and activities of these charities.

Barnardo's
Barnardo's (formerly known as Dr Barnardo's) is one of the most well-known children's charities. It was founded by Thomas Barnardo, who was born in Ireland and converted to Evangelical Christianity as a teenager. He came to London to study medicine and originally planned to become a medical missionary but was moved by the plight of homeless children there and, with the help of supporters, the first home for destitute children was opened in 1868. He continued to fundraise and open more homes including the Stepney Boy's Home, which had its own photographic department to produce 'before' and 'after' pictures for publicity and the Village Home for Girls in Ilford, a complete community of staff and children numbering over 1,000 in total. By 1878, Thomas Barnardo had helped to establish fifty orphanages all over London. It was here that a scheme for sending children to Canada was first developed, with more than 8,000 children shipped between 1882 and 1901. In addition to the ongoing residential care of children, the practice of 'boarding out' was also widely used. Thomas Barnardo encouraged the fostering of babies and children, believing that a family home was the best place to raise a child. Also, despite his strong Christian values, he was extremely forward-thinking in his beliefs about babies who were born to single women. Far from taking these babies permanently away from their 'sinful' mothers, the charity often arranged for the mother to live and work near to where the her baby was boarded out and visiting was permitted.

Thomas Barnardo died in 1905, by which time there were more than 4,000 children boarded out, 8,000 in residential care and 18,000 in total had been sent to Canada and Australia (see also Child Migrants). The work of Dr Barnardo's expanded to other parts of the country and gradually changed to focus more on adoption and the care of children with special needs. The charity thrives today and still facilitates adoption and fostering and advises on the care and welfare of children.

Barnardo's has a dedicated Family History Service, with a vast archive of records and photographs of its homes and the children who were in its care. There is a range of services to help establish if your ancestor was a Barnardo's child and provide information about them. Application is made by completing an enquiry form and a fee is payable. If your ancestor was a Barnado's child, more detailed records, including pictures, can then be requested and there is a further fee to pay for these. Full details of the services and cost can be found on the Barnardo's website under 'What We Do'.

Barnardo's
Cottage 4
Tanners Lane
Barkingside
Essex, IG6 1QG
Telephone: 020 8498 7536
Emails:**familyhistoryservice@barnardos.org.uk**
makingconnections@barnardos.org.uk (for former Barnardo's children)
Web: **www.barnardos.org.uk**

Salvation Army

William Booth founded the Salvation Army, formerly called the Christian Mission, in the East End of London in 1865. His mission was to give practical help to the poor and destitute, whilst also preaching the Gospel to them. Members were led to engage in the 'spiritual battle against the forces of sin', including alcohol, and to convert the 'fallen' to Christianity. Realising that poverty and hardship hindered their mission, the Salvation Army established centres to offer food and shelter.

The first children's homes were started by the charity in the 1880s after it became obvious that refuges set up for destitute women attracted many single expectant mothers. Dedicated 'rescue homes' were established to care for these women and their babies and arrangements for adoption were made by the charity. The last of these homes in the UK closed in the 1980s when the numbers of adoptions were declining and social attitudes to illegitimacy had changed.

The Salvation Army Heritage Centre holds original records of around a thousand adoptions between 1885 and 1933. Information about many more adoptions, however, survive in large volumes called 'Statement Books', complied from the returns of mother and baby homes where children were cared for and subsequently adopted. Although compiled mainly for statistical purposes, brief details in the form of discharge documents of around 65,000 children were recorded in the statement books. These documents contain the name of the natural mother and often give the name of another agency through which an adoption was made (whose detailed records may survive).

Information from adoption records and statement books is provided free of charge for anyone born in a Salvation Army mother and baby home, although evidence of identity will be requested. The Centre is also happy to provide transcribed extracts from their records for genealogical purposes although there is a fee. Sensitive information and details of third parties, however, may be edited to comply with current data protection legislation.

The Salvation Army International Heritage Centre
House 14
William Booth College
Champion Park
London SE5 8BQ
Tel: 020 7737 4071
Email: **heritage@salvationarmy.org.uk**
Web: **www.salvationarmy.org.uk**

Children's Society

The Children's Society was established in 1881 by Sunday school teacher, Edward Rudolf as the Church of England Central Home for Waifs and Strays. He was shocked to discover that children were begging on the streets for food and approached his Archbishop to suggest that the church should do more to help and support destitute children and their families. Within ten years there were 35 children's homes and the society started to become involved in arrangements for children in its care to be fostered and adopted. By 1905 there were almost 3,500 children under the care of the Society; most were in residential homes but almost 1,000 were fostered. The Society also became involved in the child emigration scheme and helped to send around 3,500 children to Canada, Australia and Rhodesia between 1883 and the late 1950s.

The society's name was changed to the Church of England Children's Society in 1946 and was renamed simply The Children's Society in 1982.

The Children's Society Records and Archive Centre holds records about the society and the children in its care between 1882 and 1926, including around 30,000 individual case files.

For more information:
Email: **archives@childrenssociety.org.uk**
Web: **www.hiddenlives.org.uk**

The Society also has a dedicated Post Adoption and Care Service, which holds records on 130,000 children who were cared for and adopted from the Society.

Unit 203
Block A, Floor 2, Tower Bridge Business Complex
100 Clements Road
SE16 4DG London
Tel: 020 7232 5288
Email: **postadoption@childrenssociety.org.uk**

Coram

"When Captain Coram returned from sea in 1720 he was shocked to see children abandoned or dying on London's streets. The only option for women who had children born out of wedlock with no means to support them was to be placed in a parish poorhouse, with high mortality rates. Thomas Coram began a campaign to create a home for these babies, overcoming widespread prejudice about children born outside of marriage, by enlisting the support of leading members of the aristocracy, the City, the arts and the sciences though a series of petitions…

…Thomas Coram's 19-year campaign was finally brought to the attention of King George II who signed a Royal Charter on 17 October 1739 for the creation of the Foundling Hospital, which went on to be built in Bloomsbury….

…Mothers brought their babies to the Foundling Hospital to be cared for, with many hopeful that their financial circumstances would change so they could one day reclaim them. The Hospital arranged for foster families, many in the Home Counties, to care for the babies and young children until the age of five. They were then brought to live and be educated in the Foundling Hospital until the age of 15, many being trained for domestic or military service".

From the website of the Coram Foundation (now named simply 'Coram') **www.coram.org.uk**

Although always concerned with the welfare of children in its care, the foundation was at times equally concerned with the morals of children from 'fallen women'. Infants were baptised, given new names and helped to work toward a legitimate place in society. The values of the Victorian era continued into the 20th Century but today the charity focusses on practical and emotional support for vulnerable children as well as adoption placement, support for parents and education programmes.

The historical archives of the Foundling Hospital are held by the London Metropolitan Archives:

40 Northampton Road
Clerkenwell
EC1R 0HB
Tel: 020 7332 3820
Email: **ask.lma@cityoflondon.gov.uk**
Web: **www.cityoflondon.gov.uk/things-to-do/visiting-the-city/archives-and-city-history/london-metropolitan-archives**

Coram holds birth and care records of children it raised and cared for that are made available to former residents of the foundation, or those fostered and adopted out, and their descendants. Access to these records, and specialist counselling, is offered through an experienced social worker. Contact:

Email: **adoption@coram.org.uk**
Tel: 020 7520 0383

A list of children who were in the care of the Foundling Hospital between 1853 and 1948 is also held at the General Register Office for England and Wales in Southport. Visit www.gro.gov.uk or call 0300 123 1837.

National Children's Home (originally 'The Children's Home', later NCH, now Action for Children)

This charity was formed in 1869 by Methodist minister Thomas Bowman Stephenson, who befriended children who were begging under the arches of Waterloo station. It soon grew, thanks to donations from many churchgoers and friends of Mr Stephenson, from a few residential homes in London to a national charity with many orphanages and thousands of children in its care. The child migration scheme was also supported by the charity, which sent almost 3,000 children to a centre in Ontario, Canada.

The charity branched into education in addition to care and founded schools and training establishments at various locations in England from 1875. Later, babies and young children were routinely adopted and fostered out. NCH has evolved into a thriving charity supporting children in different ways through care, education, adoption and fostering and family support.

The files survive for most of the tens of thousands of children who were cared for at any time by any part of NCH. Previous residents and surviving relatives may access the files. Most archived files are deposited at Liverpool University Special Collections and Archives, although records relating to the Frodsham Branch of the charity are deposited in the Cheshire Archives. However, these records are subject to closure rules and access restrictions so permission to view them must first be obtained from the charity.

NCH
3 The Boulevard
Ascot Road
Watford
WD18 8AG
Phone: 01923 361 500
Email: **ask.us@actionforchildren.org.uk**
www.actionforchildren.org.uk/our-services/adoption-fostering-and-children-in-care/records-and-support

Child Migrants Trust

When the practice of child migration came to light in the early 1980s, through the work of Nottingham Social Worker Margaret Humphries, the Child Migrants Trust was established to investigate the extent and practices of the child emigration policy and campaign for the rights of child migrants. More importantly the Trust offers advice, support, counselling, information and family reunion services to child migrants and their relatives. In addition to a base in the UK they have offices in Melbourne and Perth, Australia.

Child Migrants Trust
124 Musters Road
West Bridgford
Nottingham, U.K.
NG2 7PW
Tel: 0115 982 2811
Email: **enquiries@childmigrantstrust.com**
Web: **www.childmigrantstrust.com**

Independent and local authority homes

There were many thousands of independent orphanages, children's homes and 'mother and baby' homes in existence in the 19th and 20th centuries. Churches, charities and well off individuals established and ran homes for the benefit of local orphaned or destitute children, or provided a short term refuge for single women to give birth to their babies. In the mid to late 1900s many were merged, closed or became council-run homes, when the role of care for children without parents or families was gradually taken on by local authorities. Often, in the case of the mother and baby homes, the address of the institution, which can appear to be a private address, was recorded as the birthplace of the child on his or her birth certificate. Where records have survived they often ended up in the archives of the local authority responsible for the area where the home was, although policy on access varies and may be subject to restrictions. Find more information about children's homes at **http://childrenshomes.org.uk**, mother and baby homes at **www.mother andbabyhomes.com** and local authorities at **www.gov.uk/find-your-local-council** - most council websites have an A-Z list of services or a search facility. A search using the term 'archives' will usually find the correct department but if it cannot be found a call to the general enquires number is sometimes helpful.

If a close relative was adopted out
It is recommended that you first of all place your details on the Adoption Contact Register (see page 39) in case your birth relative has already done so and would be willing to hear from you.

If there is no corresponding information on the contact register, the index of the Adopted Children Register (ACR, see page 22) is a possible starting point for finding the adoptive details of your relative.

Unless the adopted name of your birth relative was known, it was previously almost impossible to find out any more about them or make contact.

Due to a recent change in legislation* adoption professionals are now able to identify your birth relatives from the ACR on your behalf and, although they will not inform you of the new name that your relative was given, they will try to contact them (or refer you to an agency who will) and act as an intermediary. If your relative wants contact they will put you in touch. Due to the heavy workload of these departments there may be a waiting list.

Contact the Adoption Section of the General Register Office (see page 46) for more information. If you want to trace and contact your relative yourself, do read the advice about sensitivity and discretion, and particularly about making an approach, in the following section for adopted people.

If your parent, grandparent or other close relative was adopted in

Until recently, if your parent or grandparent was adopted but they were now deceased, there was no provision for you to access any information about their original birth family and intermediary services were not available in circumstances such as these. The right to obtain an original birth certificate and access documents relating to an adoption was only available to an adopted person and that right died with them, meaning that children or grandchildren of an adopted person could never discover their genetic roots or have the opportunity to link up with biological relatives.

Thanks to a long campaign by the Descendants of Adopted Persons (DAP) Group, the law was amended in October 2014.* Descendants can now access intermediary services and may, through this process, gain access to some information that could help them discover information about their relative's birth family.

Find out more from the Adoption Search Reunion page on this subject at: **www.adoptionsearchreunion.org.uk/search/dap/** where you can download the 'Prescribed relatives of adopted people' guide or call Adoption Search Reunion at BAAF on 020 7421 2600.

Natural parents

If your baby was given up for adoption and you would like to find out more about them or make contact it is essential that this is done through the proper channels and with the support of professionals. Visit www.baaf.org.uk or call their Advice line on Tel:020 3597 6116. You might also find this website for natural parents helpful: **www.n-p-n.co.uk**

*The Adoption Information and Intermediary Services (Pre-Commencement Adoptions) (Amendment) Regulations 2014.

If you were adopted

Many adoptees feel that their 'real' parents are their adopters and, particularly if their upbringing was a happy one, feel they are betraying them by looking for their birth family. Reluctance to discuss the decision to search with your adoptive parents is understandable although often they expect it and may even encourage or help.

A life-changing event sometimes ignites curiosity about your natural family – getting married, the birth of your first child, the death of an adoptive parent or a life-threatening illness can lead to questions about your past and your roots. Sometimes, however, emotional problems, such as depression and anxiety, can develop without an obvious cause. This may subconsciously be connected to the time when, as an infant, you were separated from your birth mother and left with strangers. Even if you have no conscious memory of this and had a happy childhood, feelings of abandonment might continue throughout life until they are addressed. Nancy Verrier's thought provoking book, The Primal Wound, explores this in detail and many adopted people and their families have found it helpful (details in Further Reading).

Every adopted person is different, of course, and some may never have any emotional problems.

Tracing your natural family is not something to be entered into lightly. Whatever you discover it cannot be subsequently forgotten and you should not underestimate the emotional effect the search and possible reunion can have on you and your loved ones.

It is partly for this reason that adoption professionals stand between you as an adoptee and the records relating to your natural parents and the circumstances of your birth.

Access to birth records

The first step towards tracing your natural family is to identify your birth mother. You may have been given some information by your adoptive parents, but usually you will need a copy of your original birth certificate to find out the name of your mother at the time you were born. It is impossible to link an adoption record to a birth record and you cannot just order a copy of your birth certificate if you were adopted. You can apply for your original birth certificate by completing an application for Birth certificate Information Before Adoption (BIBA) form, which you can find, view and download via the following website: **www.gov.uk/adoption-records.**

If you were adopted before 1975, you will be required by law to attend an interview before you are given information about your birth and a copy of your original birth certificate. This interview is referred to as counselling and some adoptees are wary, even indignant, that this is necessary. However, this process is all in the best interests of both you and your birth mother. Women who gave children for adoption before 1975 would have been given the impression that the child would never be able to trace them, as this was the law at the time. When the law was changed to allow adoptees to look for their birth families it was thought essential that adoptees undertaking a search were aware of this and the potential distress that might be caused by a child making contact was taken into account. In addition to your original birth certificate, if records have survived you might also be able to view the original adoption papers, which will give more detailed information about your birth mother, her family background, her age and address at the time of your adoption and perhaps some information about your birth father. These documents can offer some insight into the life of your birth mother at the time and perhaps help you to understand her decision to place you for adoption.

The counselling interview, in addition to providing you with documents and discovering more about your adoption, give you the opportunity to talk about your reasons for searching and your hopes, fears and expectations.

Even if you were adopted after 1975, you will be entitled and encouraged to attend a counselling interview voluntarily. Counselling can be arranged by the Adoptions Section of the General Register Office or your local Social Services department. Every local authority has an adoption department with a section or officer who deals with post-adoption issues. Sometimes inter-mediary or counselling services are outsourced to another agency but Social Services will refer or signpost if this is the case. If you call the local authority main telephone number and ask for adoption they will be able to help, or simply type the name of the county/city and 'Adoption' to find the information online. If you now live in different area to the one where you were born or your adoption took place, records can be transferred between authorities and from the General Register Office. You may need to wait several weeks or even months for an appointment as these departments have a heavy workload and there is always a waiting list.

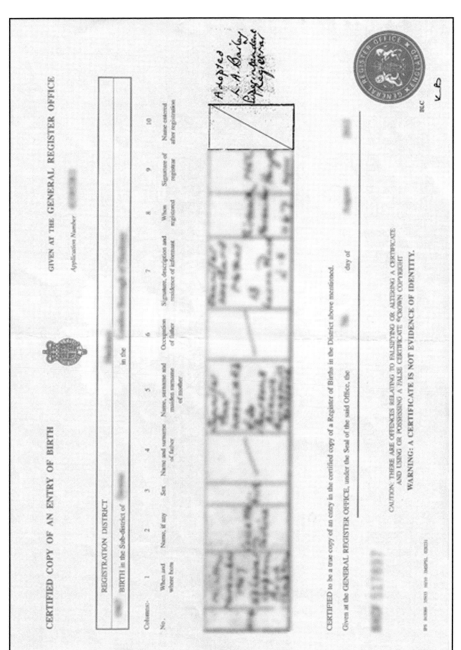

An original birth certificate, indicating that this child was adopted. © Crown copyright.

CERTIFIED COPY OF AN ENTRY IN THE RECORDS OF THE GENERAL REGISTER OFFICE

Given at the GENERAL REGISTER OFFICE

GAB 075770

Application Number

(1) No. of entry	(2) Date and country of birth of child (see footnotes)	(3) Name and surname of child	(4) Sex of child	(5) Name and surname, address and occupation of adopter or adopters	(6) Date of adoption order and description of court by which made	(7) Date of entry	(8) Signature of officer deputed by Registrar General to attest the entry

CERTIFIED copy of an entry in the Adopted Children Register maintained at the General Register Office given at the GENERAL REGISTER OFFICE, under the seal of the said Office, the

This certificate is issued pursuant to the Adoption and Children Act 2002. By Section 77(4) and (5) of the Act, a certified copy of an entry in the Adopted Children Register of purporting to be sealed or stamped with the seal of the General Register Office, is to be received as evidence of the adoption to which it relates without further or other proof; and where the entry contains a record of the date or country or district and sub-district of birth of the adopted person, such certified copy shall also be received as evidence of that date or country or district and sub-district as of respects as if the copy were a certified copy of an entry in the Registers of Births.

CAUTION: THERE ARE OFFENCES RELATING TO FALSIFYING OR ALTERING A CERTIFICATE AND USING OR POSSESSING A FALSE CERTIFICATE. CROWN COPYRIGHT

WARNING: A CERTIFICATE IS NOT EVIDENCE OF IDENTITY

An adoption certificate for the same child as above. © Crown copyright.

Case study – Tony

Tony was in his 50s when his mother passed away. His father had died when he was a baby and little Anthony was adopted by his mother's husband before he was three years old. Whist undergoing counselling for depression following the death of his mother, Tony decided that he needed to know more about his natural father. 'I didn't get along with my step-dad at all,' he explained, 'and I don't think he liked me very much. I have never even seen a photo of my real father and don't know if I have any relatives on that side of my family. I feel as though half of my history is missing and I need to know about my dad so that I can move on and live my life.'

The Adoption Contact Register

When you have your original birth certificate and have decided to search for more information, there is one step that it is important to undertake first. It is quite possible that your birth mother or other birth relatives might have been looking for you. The Adoption Contact Register at the General Register Office is the official and recommended way for birth relatives to indicate that they would like contact. Adopted people, birth parents who gave up a child for adoption and close relatives of an adoptee can apply to be placed on the register. This service can also be used to indicate that you do not want contact. If you are an adoptee you will need to know your original birth name and the name of your birth mother before you apply. There are two parts to the Register – Part 1 is for adopted people who want to connect with birth relatives and Part 2 is for birth relatives who want to connect with an adopted person. Details and an indication of wishes is added to one part of the Register and if a relative has also applied for contact on the other part of the Register then a process begins, with the consent of both parties, to put the relatives in touch with each other. Letters and photographs can also be deposited with your application if you wish.

To join the Adoption Contact Register, visit www.gov.uk/adoption-records/the-adoption-contact-register to download the relevant application form (CR1 or CR2) or call the Adoption Section on 0300 123 1837 to receive one in the post. There is a registration fee, currently £15 and £30 respectively for Part 1 and Part 2. When the registration is complete you will receive notification if there is a corresponding entry on the other part of the register and you will be told what the next steps will be.

Another contact register was operated by the adoption charity NORCAP for many years. NORCAP went into administration in January 2013 and management of the electronic information on the contact register (entries for about 60,000 individuals) was transferred to the British Association for Adoption and Fostering (BAAF) for safe keeping. At the time of writing the register is not currently active and no additions or matches can be made. Some of NORCAP's active adoption case records are currently being stored by Oxfordshire County Council www.oxfordshire.gov.uk and applications for access will only be accepted from a registered adoption support agency. For more information and the current situation regarding NORCAP's records and contact register read the information on **www.baaf.org.uk/media/norcap-contact-register-moves-baaf** or call the BAAF Helpline on 0203 597 6116 (Mon – Fri, 9am – 1pm)

Tracing Birth Relatives

Once you have your original birth certificate, information on here (and any other information you have been given from the time of your adoption) can be used to start searching. This can be done without the help of a researcher or agency but it is important to take it slowly, be very discreet in your investigations if you contact anyone for information and avoid making the initial contact yourself (see Making an approach, below). If someone else is to carry out the search for you, ensure before they begin that they have an understanding of adoption issues and that they will be mindful of the importance of discretion and respect for privacy throughout. A tactless researcher or investigator asking questions of relatives or friends of the natural mother may cause embarrassment, especially if the people in her life were not aware of your existence. If you have any problem finding someone suitable to undertake a search for you, any registered adoption support agency should be able to provide a list of approved or recommended researchers. You can search for agencies at www.adoptionsearchreunion.org.uk/help/database

It may take months for your researcher to piece together information leading to a possible current address for your birth mother or a close birth relative. This may be frustrating, and you might be impatient just to find your mother and make contact. However, to discover everything about your mother's life from the time of your adoption until the present day all at once may be difficult to come to terms with. It is best to receive or uncover information a little at a time, absorbing what has been found and reflecting for a while before continuing with further research. When you do at last have a possible address or contact details for a member of your birth family consider carefully what to do next. Someone who is experienced in these matters can increase the chances of contact being successful whereas someone who is emotionally involved or inexperienced may inadvertently jeopardise the potential relationship.

If you do decide to find your birth family yourself, be mindful that your birth may be a secret and making direct contact out of the blue is not advisable. Public records including birth, marriage and death certificates and electoral registers can be used to piece together information about your birth family from the time of your adoption. Online resources and social media sites might also help you to find links but these should be used with caution and not for direct contact. The Adoption Search Reunion website **www.adoptionsearchreunion.org.uk** is a great starting point with advice, information and links relating to searching for relatives and also information about intermediary services that can make an approach to birth relatives on your behalf.

In addition to the records detailed earlier, my book, The People Finder (see Contacts, Resources and Further Reading) has more information, resources and ideas for tracing people. This detailed guide published by the British Library also is very helpful **www.bl.uk/reshelp/findhelprestype/offpubs/electreg/traceliv/tracinglivingpeople.pdf** and more online resources are listed at the end of this book.

Making an approach

Before contacting your birth mother or other relatives, it is important to consider all possible outcome scenarios and try to be prepared. Ensure that you have plenty of support and take things slowly. Approaches via social media, or by turning up at someone's home can be a recipe for disaster and must be avoided, however tempting. You must give your relative the time and space to think and respond in their own time. It is also important to respect their privacy, not disclose information about your birth to other relatives and try not to harass or pester, even if you do not receive a response immediately.

The best way to make a first approach to a birth relative is by letter, preferably through a professional intermediary (see above). If you do decide to make contact yourself (or ask a relative or friend to do so), your initial letter should be carefully and discreetly worded in case other people in your relative's immediate family do not know about you. Keep it short and provide as many options for contacting you as possible. Be patient and let your relative decide how things progress.

Additional Case Studies

Case Study 1 – A deceased father who was adopted

Mary Cane married Raymond Matthews in the summer of 1962. Within five years they had two daughters. Mary always knew that Raymond was adopted but her husband showed little interest in finding out more – he had been lucky to be adopted by a lovely couple, a policeman and his wife, and had a very happy childhood.

Sadly, in 1938, when Raymond was just 32 years old, he died suddenly from a brain haemorrhage. When their daughters were older they became interested in finding out more about their father and his family of origin. Mary had very little information and only one document – Raymond's adoption certificate. She knew that he was born in London but nothing more about his life before his adoption. She tried several avenues over the course of two years in an attempt to help them but, time after time, was unsuccessful. She says "I wrote to all of the adoption charities that had homes in the area where he was born, approached the adoptions section of the General Register Office and searched indexes covering his date of birth but nothing was working. Whoever I approached told me that only my husband was entitled to information about his birth parents and, as he was deceased, they could not tell me anything. It was very frustrating". The breakthrough came one day with a call to the London Metropolitan Archives. She was lucky to get through to someone helpful, who agreed to look in the court records for the date when Raymond was adopted. It was confirmed, when Mary gave her husband's adopted name, that there was a file with documents relating to his adoption. Due to Data Protection legislation, no information from the file could be given to Mary, as there were procedures that had to be followed, but it was a start. The next step was an appointment with an adoption support worker at the local Social Services, who could apply to the LMA for a copy of the adoption file. Mary attended an interview, accompanied by her daughters, where they explained that they wanted to learn more about their father because they found it difficult not knowing anything, even his medical history, as they had been very young when he died. The Social Worker showed them a copy of Raymond's original birth certificate, which recorded that his birth name was Graham White and his mother was Martha White, a cook who lived in Salisbury. No details about the father were given. This was interesting but the girls wanted to know more. It was agreed that a copy of the court file would be obtained and after a few months, another meeting was arranged so that they could view the documents and discuss the contents of the file. "We found out quite a lot more about Graham's parents and, surprisingly, there were letters from both his mother and father" said Mary. They learned that Graham's father was William Smith from Exeter and Martha had moved to Devon, presumably to work. Both had written letters to the court to state that they understood they were surrendering any parental rights and wished the adoption order to be granted. With this information, more could be discovered about the backgrounds of Raymond's parents and their families. Research is still in progress but it has already been discovered that Martha was most likely a widow and William was a married man. "My daughters are looking forward to finding out more", says Mary, "and perhaps meeting with blood relatives of their father one day".

Case Study 2 – A childless couple taking in a local orphan
Alberta Ford was born in Dickleburgh, Norfolk, in 1869, the daughter of James Ford, a butcher, and his wife Mary. Alberta was the youngest of four children and by the end of 1871, her mother and an older sister had died. Although there is no record of her father's death, at the time of the 1881 census she was aged 12 and described as an 'adopted child' living with the Garland family in Dickleburgh. Arthur and Charlotte Garland were both born in Dickleburgh and had no children of their own. In 1881 they were aged 36 and 34 respectively and Arthur was described as a cattle dealer. Alberta's older sister, Margaret, was recorded lodging with a Mrs Turner just a few doors away. , When Alberta married Robert Murrell in 1890 it was stated that her father, James Ford, was deceased but her brother, William James Ford, was one of the witnesses. It appears that Mr and Mrs Garland continued to be involved with Alberta and her family after marriage and also took in another child. At the time of the 1901 census, Alberta's son, George Murrell, was staying with them and was described as their 'grandson'. They also had a girl called Florence Garland in the house, who was described as their 'adopted daughter'.

From 1891 to 1911 inclusive, the Garlands also employed a domestic servant, so it would appear that taking in children who were not related to them was genuine adoption, rather than for the purposes of engaging home help. The fact Alberta's son not only lived with them as a child but also later followed his 'grandfather' into the family business of cattle dealing, is an indication of the ongoing connection between the two families.

Case Study 3 – Liz P's adoption
Liz was adopted as a baby but traced her mother several years ago. She understands completely the reason why she was given up for adoption and that her mother had no choice. Liz's father was a married man with whom her mother had an affair. She says "My birth mother still feels shame about having a baby out of wedlock and therefore has only revealed my existence to a handful of trusted people. She had several siblings (who have all died over the last few years) but none of them knew anything about my existence. If they ever had suspected that my mother had had a baby and given it up for adoption they could have searched the GRO birth index and the evidence of my birth, at least, would have been there. Clearly, however, none of them had any reason to look."

Liz says of her biological father – "I've never been particularly interested in him. Although I have been told his name I can honestly say that can't remember it, which is probably an indication of how unimportant he is to me. I do have his name written down somewhere but am not concerned that I can't remember where and have no inclination to trace him. He is almost certainly dead by now, or at least in his 90s, and any other children he had are probably going to be even older than me (I'm 53). To me there is little point in sullying any memory of their father by revealing that he not only had an affair but also unknowingly fathered a child.

My children, however, have occasionally mentioned him and rightly say there may be medical history that could be relevant to them. I guess if they were showing any signs of an inherited illness and knowing their genetic inheritance could help them I'd possibly be keener to trace him or any of his descendants and could possibly get more information from my birth mother, although I realise that there is a time limit on this."

Case Study 4 – Christine Wibberley's grandmother
A fascinating and detailed account of researcher Christine Wibberley's grandmother, Margaret, the birth of her illegitimate daughter, Mollie, (Christine's mother) and the circumstances under which her child was raised, appears on Christine's website: **www.christinewibberley.co.uk/one-of-my-ancestors**

In this true-life story with echoes of Downton Abbey, a senior domestic servant in a large household fell pregnant in 1907. This could have been a disastrous event (and indeed was so for many in her position during that era), but Margaret had the good fortune to find a well-to-do childless couple to raise her daughter and continued in her career well into her sixties, rising with each workplace move to a higher position. She maintained contact with her daughter, leaving her the bulk of her estate when she died a relatively wealthy spinster in 1943. The identity of Mollie's father was never revealed.

Contacts, Resources and Further Reading

Adoptions Section, General Register Office
Room C201
General Register Office
Trafalgar Road
SOUTHPORT
PR8 2HH
Tel 0151 471 4830 (9am to 5pm Monday to Friday)
Email: **adoptions@gro.gsi.gov.uk**

The National Records of Scotland Adoption Unit
Room 3
General Register House
2 Princes Street
Edinburgh
EH1 3YY
Telephone: 0131 535 1355, 1383 or 1376

British Association of Adoption and Fostering (BAAF)
Saffron House,
6-10 Kirby Street,
London,
EC1N 8TS
Tel 020 7421 2600
Email: **mail@baaf.org.uk**
Web: **www.baaf.org.uk** and **www.adoptionsearchreunion.org.uk**

Post Adoption Centre
5 Torriano Mews
Torriano Avenue
London NW5 2RZ
Tel: 020 7284 0555
Web: **www.pac-uk.org**

After Adoption
Unit 5 Citygate
5 Blantyre Street
Castlefield
Manchester
M15 4JJ
Email: **information@afteradoption.org.uk**
Tel: 0800 0 568 578

The People Finder: Reuniting Relatives, Finding Friends, Karen Bali, Nicholas Brealey Publishing, 2007.

New Cousins: How to Trace Living Descendants of your Ancestors (2nd edition), The Family History Partnership, 2012

The Adoption Reunion Handbook, Elizabeth Trinder and others, John Wiley & Sons, 2005, ISBN: 9780470094228.

Children Under the Poor Law, W. Chance, Swann Sonnenschein & Co., 1897.

A Child for Keeps: the History of Adoption in England, 1918-45, Jenny Keating, Palgrave Macmillan, 2007, ISBN: 9780230517882.

How to research childhoods spent in former children's homes, orphanages, cottage homes and other children's institutions, Gudrun Jane Limbrick, WoodWorks, 2013, ISBN: 9781903210291.

Leaving the workhouse: the story of Victorian orphanages, Gudrun Jane Limbrick, WordWorks, 2014, ISBN: 978-1-903210-26-0.

The Primal Wound: Understanding the adopted child , Nancy Verrier , British Association for Adoption and Fostering, 2009

Coming Home to Self: Healing the Primal Wound, Nancy Verrier, self published, 2003, ISBN: 1905664761.

Journey of the Adopted Self: A Search for Wholeness, Betty Jean Lifton, Basic Books, 1995.

Tracing Birth Relatives: A practical guide for adopted people, BAAF (British Association for Adoption and Fostering) 2010.

Philanthropy and Community: Children in Care in Dickleburgh, Norfolk, 1875-1912, Rosemary Steer, University of Dundee, 2014 (Dissertation).

Baby Farmers of the 19th Century (Female Killers series), Sylvia Perrini, Goldmineguides.com, 2013. ISBN: 9781484128725.

Oranges and Sunshine, (a book, formerly titled 'Empty Cradles' and later also made into a film about Child Migrants), Margaret Humphries, Corgi, 2011, ISBN : 9780552163354.

Lost Children of the Empire, Philip Bean and Joy Melville, Unwin Hyman, 1989 (out of print)

A History of Adoption in England and Wales (1850-1961), Gill Rossini, Pen & Sword Books Ltd, 2014 ISBN: 9781781593950

www.foundlingmuseum.org.uk

www.childrenscottagehomes.org.uk

www.childrenshomes.org.uk

www.theirhistory.co.uk (Information, history and personal stories about NCH)

www.motherandbabyhomes.com

www.ffhs.org.uk/tips/adoption.php

https://motherandbabyhomes.wordpress.com

www.n-p-n.co.uk